CAJUN
COOKING

Editor:
Valerie Ferguson

LORENZ BOOKS

Contents

Introduction

In the 17th century, French settlers arrived in Nova Scotia, Canada, bringing their own hearty country style of cooking with them. This is where Cajun cuisine began. When they moved south to Louisiana in the 18th century, they adapted their cooking techniques to the local ingredients: seafood, wild fowl, game, wild vegetables and herbs.

Creole cuisine, however, grew up in New Orleans. It was city food, sophisticated for the wealthy Europeans who had established plantations in Louisiana. Their cooks, often from Africa, combined the European style with indigenous ingredients and their own culinary traditions, using ingredients such as corn, cayenne and okra.

By the mid 20th century, Cajun and Creole cooking had merged, particularly in the many restaurants. New Louisiana cuisine includes plenty of black and white peppercorns, not available to the original cooks, as well as the local spices. With modern fast cooking came a new technique, called blackening: chicken or fish is covered with spices and fast fried. This method has become a cornerstone of Cajun cuisine.

Modern Cajun cooking retains its original message – to be adventurous with whatever is good and fresh. These recipes are just that.

Ingredients

Cajun cooking may be characterized by its ability to adapt all available ingredients, but they are invariably of the freshest and highest quality.

Vegetables

With its farming ancestry, Cajun cooking features a wide range of fresh vegetables. The trio of onion, celery and green (bell) peppers is classic, appearing in many recipes. Spring greens (collards) and Chinese leaves (Chinese cabbage) are used extensively, but other greens such as green cabbage, kale and spinach are also frequently used. New World vegetables, such as sweet potatoes and ordinary potatoes, tomatoes and okra, were quickly 'colonized', and chillies are at the centre of Cajun cuisine. Corn is widely used, both as a vegetable, as flour for coating food for frying and ground to make cornmeal. Refrigerated transportation has

Above: Shellfish is an integral part of cooking in Louisiana.

extended the range to include many Old World vegetables, such as artichokes and aubergines (eggplant).

Fish & Seafood

The Mississippi, the bayous and the Gulf of Mexico provide a wealth of freshwater and sea fish. Red snapper, known as redfish, and dog fish are probably the most popular varieties. Favourite shellfish include prawns (shrimp), lobster, crab, oysters and clams. Freshwater crayfish is a speciality of the region.

Meat & Poultry

The pig was the most important farm animal, not least because just about every part of it is edible. Besides pork, bacon, gammon and ham feature in

Below: A sauté of onions and chopped peppers is the base of many Cajun dishes.

many Cajun recipes. Lard was the preferred cooking fat, although corn oil can be substituted. Chicken and poussins are also widely used.

Rice
Long grain rice is popular in Cajun cooking, and an intrinsic ingredient in Jambalaya and Dirty Rice. It is also served with Gumbo or as a side dish.

Fresh Fruit
Cranberries are probably the most widely used native fruit in the region and many other fruits, particularly oranges, lemons and coconuts are used in both sweet and savoury dishes.

Nuts
Pecan nuts are synonymous with America's Deep South where they grow in abundance. They are used with both sweet and savoury dishes. Walnuts too, are used in Cajun cooking.

Below: Cranberries are often used to make a sauce to accompany a dessert.

Spices & Seasonings
The essential combination is plenty of salt, freshly ground black and white pepper and cayenne. The latter is made from the finely ground pods and seeds of one of the most pungent varieties of chilli and should be used with caution. Tabasco sauce, made from hot red peppers and vinegar, was invented in Louisiana. Dijon mustard is also a regular addition to many recipes. Cumin and sweet paprika, are frequently used, and warm, sweet spices such as cinnamon, nutmeg and allspice are used in many dishes.

Fresh Herbs
Many varieties are essential to the flavour of Cajun cooking, but the most popular are basil, parsley and oregano. They are added during the cooking process and as colourful garnishes. The pungent aromatic, garlic, is also frequently used to flavour dishes.

Below: Pecan nuts have a deliciously rich buttery taste.

Techniques

De-veining

When using raw prawns (jumbo shrimp) remove the black vein.

1 Holding the raw prawn in one hand, pull off the legs with the fingers of the other. Pull off the head.

2 Peel off the body shell. When you reach the tail, hold the body and firmly pull the tail; the shell will come off with it.

3 Make a shallow cut along the centre of the prawn's back. Pull out and discard the black vein using the tip of the knife.

4 Rinse briefly under cold water and pat dry with kitchen paper.

Skinning Tomatoes

This is a very simple and easy way to prepare tomatoes for cooking.

1 Using a small sharp knife, cut a small cross on the base of each tomato.

2 Put the tomatoes in a bowl and pour over boiling water. Leave for 2–3 minutes until the skins split. Drain and transfer to a bowl of cold water to cool. Peel off the skins.

COOK'S TIP: Wherever possible, use fresh, ripe tomatoes with a full flavour, such as vine-ripened or plum tomatoes.

Grinding Spices

Some spices are used whole, but where they are crushed or ground, it is best to crush them as required.

1 Crush whole spices in a coffee grinder or spice mill.

2 Alternatively, use a pestle and mortar, especially for small quantities.

Making a Roux

This thickening agent is a crucial ingredient in many Cajun dishes.

1 Heat the oil in a pan. When it is hot, add the flour and stir constantly with a wooden spoon until it reaches a pale brown or peanut-butter brown colour, according to the recipe. Do not let dark flecks appear as this will impair the flavour.

Chopping Garlic

Garlic is an essential flavouring for many dishes and is frequently used in Cajun cookery. It can be crushed using a garlic press or by the method below.

1 Break off the clove of garlic from the bulb, place the flat side of a large knife on top of the clove and strike it with your fist. Remove all the papery outer skin. Begin by finely chopping the clove.

2 Sprinkle over a little table salt and, using the flat side of a large knife blade, work the salt into the chopped garlic, until the clove softens and releases its aromatic juices. Use the garlic paste as required.

Creole Onion Soup

Low, slow cooking gives onions a rich, almost sweet, flavour, enhanced in this soup by a shot of bourbon.

Serves 4

INGREDIENTS
50 g/2 oz/¼ cup butter
2 large onions, quartered and
    thinly sliced
1 bay leaf
45 ml/3 tbsp plain (all-purpose) flour
1 litre/1¾ pints/4 cups chicken stock
75 g/3 oz/¾ cup grated
    Cheddar cheese
30 ml/2 tbsp bourbon
120 ml/4 fl oz/½ cup milk
salt and freshly ground
    black pepper

2 Sprinkle in the flour and stir until amalgamated, then remove from the heat and gradually stir in 250 ml/ 8 fl oz/1 cup of the stock. Return to the heat and stir until thickened and smooth. Add 50 g/2 oz/½ cup of the cheese and stir gently until melted.

1 Melt the butter in a deep pan and cook the onions and bay leaf, covered, over a very low heat for about 20 minutes, until very soft and pale gold, stirring occasionally.

COOK'S TIP: The onions must not be allowed to brown. Keep the heat as low as possible.

3 Gradually stir in the remaining stock and bring to the boil. Partially cover and simmer for 20 minutes.

4 Add the bourbon and return to a simmer. Cook for 1 minute, then stir in the milk and return to a simmer again. Remove the bay leaf and season to taste.

5 Ladle the soup into warmed individual bowls and scatter with the remaining Cheddar. Serve immediately while hot.

VARIATIONS: You could use other cheeses for this dish such as Gruyère. To make the dish vegetarian use vegetable stock instead of chicken.

11

Corn & Crab Bisque

This Louisiana classic is certainly luxurious enough for a dinner party. Ask the fishmonger to clean the crab, if you prefer.

Serves 8

INGREDIENTS
4 large corn cobs
3 litres/5¼ pints/13¼ cups water
2 bay leaves
1 cooked crab, about 1 kg/2¼ lb
25 g/1 oz/2 tbsp butter
30 ml/2 tbsp plain (all purpose) flour
300 ml/½ pint/1¼ cups whipping cream
6 spring onions (scallions), shredded
salt, freshly ground black and white
    pepper and cayenne pepper

1 Strip off and reserve the kernels of the corn cobs. Put the cobs into a deep pan and add the water, bay leaves and 10 ml/2 tsp salt. Bring to the boil, then simmer over a low heat while you prepare the crab.

2 Pull away the two flaps between the big claws, stand the crab on its 'nose' where the flaps were and bang down firmly with the heel of your hand on the rounded end.

3 Separate the crab from its top shell, reserving the shell. Push out the mouth and the greyish-white abdominal sac immediately below, and discard.

4 Pull away the grey feathery gills surrounding the central chamber and discard. Scrape out all the brown meat from the shell and reserve. Crack the claws and extract the white meat. Pick out the white meat from the legs and the cavities in the central body. Set all the crab meat aside.

5 Put the legs, back shell and all the other pieces of shell into the pan with the corn cobs. Simmer for a further 15 minutes, then strain the stock into a clean pan. Boil vigorously until reduced to 2 litres/3½ pints/9 cups.

COOK'S TIP: To strip the kernels from a corn cob, hold the cob upright on a board and cut downwards with a sharp, heavy knife.

6 Meanwhile, melt the butter in a small pan and sprinkle in the flour. Stir constantly over a low heat until the roux is golden brown colour. Remove from the heat and gradually stir in 250 ml/8 fl oz/1 cup of the stock. Return to the heat and stir until thickened, then stir this mixture into the remaining stock.

7 Add the corn kernels to the soup, return to the boil and simmer for 5 minutes. Add the prepared crab meat, cream and shredded spring onions and season with salt, freshly ground black pepper and cayenne pepper to taste. Return to the boil and simmer for a further 2 minutes. Serve the bisque immediately.

Hot Parsnip Fritters on Baby Spinach

Fritters are a natural favourite with Cajun cooks, with their love of deep-frying. The technique brings out the luscious sweetness of the parsnips. Served on a bed of spinach, these fritters make an unusual starter.

Serves 4

INGREDIENTS
2 large parsnips, peeled
115 g/4 oz/1 cup plain (all-purpose) flour
1 egg separated
120 ml/4 fl oz/½ cup milk
oil, for deep-frying
115 g/4 oz baby spinach leaves
30 ml/2 tbsp olive oil
15 ml/1 tbsp walnut oil
15 ml/1 tbsp sherry vinegar
15 ml/1 tbsp coarsely chopped walnuts
salt, freshly ground black pepper and
  cayenne pepper

2 Sift the flour into a bowl, make a well in the centre and add the egg yolk. Mix with a fork, gradually incorporating the flour from the sides. Begin adding the milk, while continuing to mix in the flour. Season with salt, pepper and cayenne and beat with a whisk until smooth.

3 Heat the oil for deep-frying. Meanwhile, put the spinach leaves into a bowl. Put the olive oil, walnut oil and vinegar in a screw-top jar and season with salt and pepper. Shake vigorously, then add to the spinach leaves and toss. Arrange the spinach on four plates and scatter with walnuts.

1 Put the parsnips in a pan of lightly salted water, bring to the boil and simmer for 10–15 minutes, until just tender. Drain, cool and cut diagonally into slices about 5 cm/2 in long and 5 mm–1 cm/¼–½ in thick.

4 Whisk the egg white until soft peaks form. Fold a little of the batter into the egg white, then fold the mixture into the batter.

5 Dip the parsnip slices into the batter and fry, a few at a time, until puffy and golden. Drain on kitchen paper and keep warm. Divide the fritters among the plates and serve.

VARIATION: If baby spinach is not available use crisp lettuce leaves.

Sweetcorn Cakes with Grilled Tomatoes

Use the freshest possible ingredients, so that both the corn and the tomatoes, preferably sun-ripened, retain their natural sweetness.

Serves 4

INGREDIENTS
1 large corn cob
75 g/3 oz/⅔ cup plain (all-purpose)
    flour
1 egg
a little milk
2 large, firm tomatoes
1 garlic clove, crushed
5 ml/1 tsp dried oregano
30–45 ml/2–3 tbsp vegetable oil,
    plus extra for frying
8 iceberg lettuce leaves
salt and freshly ground black pepper
shredded fresh basil leaves,
    to garnish

1 Using a sharp knife, strip the kernels from the corn cobs and put them in a pan of boiling water. Bring back to the boil and cook for 3 minutes. Drain, rinse under cold water and drain again. Set aside.

2 Sift the flour into a bowl, make a well in the centre and add the egg. Gradually stir in the flour with a fork, adding a little milk to make a soft, dropping consistency. Stir in the corn kernels and season.

3 Preheat the grill (broiler). Halve the tomatoes horizontally and make two or three criss-cross slashes across the cut sides. Rub the crushed garlic, dried oregano and salt and pepper over the cut surfaces, then drizzle with oil. Grill (broil) until lightly browned.

VARIATION: These fritters are also great served with chicken that has been tossed in seasoned flour, egg and breadcrumbs and deep-fried.

4 Heat some oil in a frying pan and drop 15 ml/1 tbsp of batter into the centre. Cook over a low heat, turning when the top has set. Drain on kitchen paper and keep warm while you cook seven more. Divide the lettuce among four plates and top with two corn cakes. Garnish with basil and serve with a tomato half.

Oyster & Bacon Brochettes

Six oysters per serving make a good starter or increase the ration to nine and serve with a salad for a light lunch.

Serves 4–6

INGREDIENTS
36 oysters
18 thin-cut rashers (strips) rindless
   streaky (fatty) bacon
115 g/4 oz/1 cup plain (all-purpose)
   flour
15 ml/1 tbsp paprika
5 ml/1 tsp cayenne pepper
5 ml/1 tsp salt
5 ml/1 tsp garlic salt
10 ml/2 tsp dried oregano
oil, for frying
celery leaves and fresh red chillies,
   to garnish

FOR THE SAUCE
½ fresh red chilli, seeded and very
   finely chopped
2 spring onions (scallions), very
   finely chopped
30 ml/2 tbsp chopped fresh parsley
juice of ¼–½ lemon
salt and freshly ground black pepper

1 Shuck the oysters over a bowl to catch their juices. Wrap one hand in a clean dish towel and cup the deep shell of one oyster. Work the point of a strong, short-bladed knife into the hinge between the shells and twist. Push the knife in and work it to cut the muscle that holds the shell closed. Tip the juices into the bowl.

2 Cut under the flesh of the oyster to free it from the shell. Drop the oyster into the bowl with the juice. Repeat with the remaining oysters and discard the drained shells.

3 Cut the bacon rashers in half across widthways and wrap each oyster in half a rasher. Thread the wrapped oysters on to four or six skewers.

4 To make the sauce, mix the fresh red chilli, finely chopped spring onions and fresh parsley into the bowl of oyster juices and add lemon juice and seasoning to taste. Transfer to a small bowl.

5 Combine the plain flour, paprika, cayenne pepper, salt, garlic salt and dried oregano, and add freshly ground black pepper to taste. Spread out the seasoned flour on a large plate and roll the skewered oysters in it, shaking off any surplus.

6 Heat 2.5 cm/1 in depth of oil in a wide frying pan and fry the skewers, in batches, over a medium heat, turning frequently, for 3–4 minutes, until they are brown all over. Drain on kitchen paper and serve with the sauce, garnished with celery leaves and chillies.

19

Seafood, Artichoke & Red Onion Salad

Artichokes are a very popular Louisiana ingredient – and the local cooks use canned hearts in the best of circles. This fresh-tasting salad can also be served with crusty bread for a light lunch for two people.

Serves 4

INGREDIENTS
1 garlic clove
10 ml/2 tsp Dijon mustard
60 ml/4 tbsp red wine vinegar
150 ml/¼ pint/⅔ cup olive oil
45 ml/3 tbsp shredded fresh
    basil leaves or 30 ml/2 tbsp finely chopped
    fresh parsley
1 red onion, very thinly sliced
350 g/12 oz cooked peeled prawns
    (shrimp)
400 g/14 oz can artichoke
    hearts, drained
½ iceberg lettuce
salt and freshly ground black pepper

2 Mix the garlic and mustard to a paste, then beat in the vinegar and olive oil to make a thick, creamy dressing. Season with salt and pepper to taste.

3 Stir the basil or parsley into the dressing, followed by the sliced red onion. Set aside at room temperature for 30 minutes.

4 Stir the prawns into the dressing, then chill in the fridge for 1 hour, or until ready to serve.

COOK'S TIP: For the best flavour, buy fresh, cooked prawns either already peeled or in their shells; they are easy to peel. Frozen peeled prawns have lost most of their flavour and are best avoided.

1 Chop the garlic, then crush it to a pulp with 5 ml/1 tsp salt, using the flat of a heavy knife blade.

5 Cut the artichoke hearts in half and finely shred the lettuce. Make a bed of lettuce on a serving platter or individual plates and scatter the artichoke hearts over it.

6 Pour the marinated prawns and dressing over the top and serve the salad immediately.

Creole Fish Stew

This simple and attractive dish is as well suited to a dinner-party menu as it is to a family supper. If possible, start preparations the evening before so that the fish will have plenty of time to marinate.

Serves 4-6

INGREDIENTS
2 red bream or large snapper, cleaned
    and cut into 2.5 cm/1 in pieces
30 ml/2 tbsp Creole spice seasoning
30 ml/2 tbsp malt vinegar
plain (all-purpose) flour, for dusting
vegetable oil, for frying
fresh oregano sprigs,
    to garnish

FOR THE SAUCE
30 ml/2 tbsp vegetable oil
15 g/½ oz/1 tbsp butter
1 onion, finely chopped
275 g/10 oz tomatoes, peeled and
    finely chopped
2 garlic cloves, crushed
2 fresh thyme sprigs
600 ml/1 pint/2½ cups fish stock
    or water
2.5 ml/½ tsp ground cinnamon
1 fresh hot red chilli, chopped
115 g/4 oz each red and green (bell)
    pepper, finely chopped
salt

1 Place the pieces of fish in a large, non-metallic dish. Add the spice seasoning and vinegar and turn to coat. Set aside to marinate for at least 2 hours or overnight in the fridge.

2 Spread out the flour on a plate and coat the marinated fish pieces in it, shaking off any excess. Heat a little oil in a large frying pan and fry the fish for about 5 minutes, until golden brown. Set aside. Don't worry if it is not yet cooked through.

3 To make the sauce, heat the oil and butter in a large frying pan and stir-fry the chopped onion for 5 minutes. Add the tomatoes, garlic and thyme, stir well and simmer for 5 minutes. Stir in the fish stock or water, cinnamon and chilli.

4 Add the fish and chopped peppers to the sauce. Simmer until the fish is cooked through and the sauce has thickened. Adjust the seasoning with salt and serve hot, garnished with fresh oregano sprigs.

COOK'S TIP: To make Creole spice seasoning, combine 15 ml/1 tbsp garlic granules, 7.5 ml/1½ tsp coarse-grain black pepper, 7.5 ml/1½ tsp paprika, 7.5 ml/1½ tsp celery salt, 7.5 ml/1½ tsp curry powder and 5 ml/1 tsp caster sugar. Store in a dry container.

Trout Meunière with Pecan Butter

The spicy Louisiana version of the classic French dish is a perfect example of this versatile cuisine, served here with a delicious nut butter.

Serves 4

INGREDIENTS
4 large trout fillets
10 ml/2 tsp paprika
5 ml/1 tsp cayenne pepper
5 ml/1 tsp dried oregano
pinch of dried thyme
2.5 ml/½ tsp garlic salt
5 ml/1 tsp salt
1 egg
120 ml/4 fl oz/½ cup milk
45 ml/3 tbsp plain (all-purpose) flour
vegetable oil, for frying
freshly ground black pepper

FOR THE PECAN BUTTER
50 g/2 oz/⅓ cup shelled
   pecan halves
50 g/2 oz/¼ cup unsalted butter
10 ml/2 tsp Worcestershire sauce
5 ml/1 tsp lemon juice

1 First, make the pecan butter. Preheat the oven to 180°C/350°F/ Gas 4. Spread out the pecans on a baking sheet and roast in the oven for 15–20 minutes. Set aside to cool.

VARIATION: This nut butter could also be served on steamed vegetables such as broccoli or courgettes.

2 Transfer the pecans to a food processor or blender and process until quite finely chopped. Add the butter, Worcestershire sauce and lemon juice and process until combined. Scrape the pecan butter on to clear film or foil, roll into a column and chill until required.

3 Rinse the trout fillets and pat dry. Remove any remaining bones.

4 Combine the paprika, cayenne, oregano, thyme, garlic salt and salt in a small bowl and add black pepper to taste. Sprinkle a pinch or two over each fillet.

5 Lightly beat together the egg and milk in a shallow dish and beat in 5 ml/1 tsp of the seasoning mix.

6 Combine the flour and the remaining seasoning mix in another shallow dish.

7 Heat the oil in a frying pan. Coat the fish first in the egg mixture and then in the seasoned flour, shaking off any excess. Fry the fillets, in batches if necessary, then drain on kitchen paper and keep warm. Unwrap the chilled butter and cut into slices about the thickness of a coin. Serve the fillets with a slice of pecan butter on each.

Blackened Redfish

A really heavy, flat-based frying pan and plenty of ventilation in the kitchen are essentials for preparing this wonderful dish.

Serves 2

INGREDIENTS
2 red snapper fillets, at least 2 cm/¾ in
    thick, thawed if frozen
75 g/3 oz/6 tbsp butter
5 ml/1 tsp paprika
2.5 ml/½ tsp dried oregano
1.5 ml/¼ tsp salt
pinch of garlic salt
pinch of cayenne pepper
freshly ground black pepper
lime slices or lemon wedges, to garnish
mixed salad, to serve

2 Melt the butter in a small pan and swirl in the paprika, oregano, salt, garlic salt, cayenne and black pepper to taste. Pour the seasoned butter over the fish, turning to coat. Keep the fish coated on both sides until you cook it.

1 Pat the fish fillets dry with kitchen paper and put them on a plate.

COOK'S TIP: The same names are often used for completely different fish in different countries. The redfish used here is red snapper, rather than the North Atlantic deepwater fish of the same name.

3 Heat a heavy-based, cast-iron frying pan over a medium heat for about 5 minutes, until it smokes and develops a grey-white patina. Turn the fillets once more in the butter, then put them, skin-side down, into the pan. Cook, pressing down regularly with a fish slice, for 2 minutes, or until the skin is crisp and very dark.

4 Pour a little of the seasoned butter over the top of each fillet and turn them over. Cook for a further 2 minutes, pressing down with the fish slice as before.

5 Serve on hot plates, with the remaining seasoned butter poured over, garnished with lime slices or lemon wedges and accompanied by a mixed salad.

Louisiana Seafood Gumbo

Gumbo is a soup, but is served over rice as a main course. In Louisiana, oysters would feature in this dish, but mussels have been substituted here.

Serves 6

INGREDIENTS

450 g/1 lb live mussels, scrubbed
    and bearded
250 ml/8 fl oz/1 cup water
450 g/1 lb raw prawns (jumbo shrimp)
1 cooked crab, about 1 kg/2¼ lb
1 small bunch of fresh parsley, leaves
    chopped and stalks reserved
150 ml/¼ pint/⅔ cup vegetable oil
115 g/4 oz/1 cup plain (all-purpose)
    flour
1 green (bell) pepper, seeded and
    chopped
1 large onion, chopped
2 celery sticks, sliced
3 garlic cloves, finely chopped
75 g/3 oz smoked spiced sausage,
    skinned and sliced
6 spring onions (scallions), shredded
Tabasco sauce
salt and cayenne pepper
boiled rice, to serve

1 Discard any mussels that are damaged or that do not shut when tapped with the back of a knife. Bring the water to the boil in a deep pan. Add the mussels, cover tightly and cook for 3 minutes over a high heat, shaking the pan from time to time, until the shells are open. If any mussels remain shut after 1 further minute's cooking, discard them.

2 Remove the mussels and discard the shells. Return the cooking liquid from the bowl to the pan and make up the quantity to 2 litres/3½ pints/9 cups with water. Peel the prawns and put the shells and heads in the pan. Remove all the meat from the crab, separating the brown and white meat. Add all the pieces of shell to the pan with 10 ml/2 tsp salt.

3 Bring the shellfish stock to the boil, skimming frequently to remove the froth that rises to the surface. When no more froth rises, add the parsley stalks and simmer for 15 minutes. Remove from the heat, cool and then strain, discarding the contents of the strainer. Make the stock up to 2 litres/3½ pints/9 cups with water.

4 Make a roux by heating the oil in a large pan. Add the flour and cook over a low heat, beating constantly with a wooden spoon or whisk until it turns golden brown.

5 Immediately, add the pepper, onion, celery and garlic and cook for about 3 minutes, until soft. Add the sausage and reheat the stock.

6 Stir the brown crab meat into the roux, then ladle in the hot stock, a little at a time, stirring constantly until fully incorporated. Bring to just below boiling point, partially cover and simmer for 30 minutes.

7 Add the prawns, mussels, white crab meat and spring onions. Bring back to the boil and season to taste with Tabasco sauce, salt and cayenne pepper. Simmer for a further minute, until the prawns are cooked and all the ingredients are piping hot.

8 Add the chopped parsley leaves and serve immediately, ladling the gumbo over hot rice in soup plates.

Seafood Creole

As sure as the Mississippi flows into the Gulf of Mexico, there'll be a seafood Creole on the Friday lunch tables of Louisiana.

Serves 6–8

INGREDIENTS

75 g/3 oz/6 tbsp unsalted butter
1 large onion, halved and thinly sliced
1 large green (bell) pepper, halved, seeded and very thinly sliced
2 celery sticks, thinly sliced
2 garlic cloves, thinly sliced
1 bay leaf
30 ml/2 tbsp paprika
450 g/1 lb tomatoes, peeled and chopped
250 ml/8 fl oz/1 cup tomato juice
20 ml/4 tsp Worcestershire sauce
4–6 dashes of Tabasco sauce
7.5 ml/1½ tsp cornflour (cornstarch)
75 ml/5 tbsp water
1.3 kg/3 lb raw prawns (jumbo shrimp), peeled and deveined
salt
boiled rice, garnished with chopped fresh parsley and shredded lemon peel, to serve (optional)

2 Add the paprika, tomatoes, tomato juice, Worcestershire sauce and Tabasco to taste. Bring to the boil and simmer until the volume has reduced by about a quarter and the vegetables are soft. Season with salt.

1 Melt 25 g/1 oz/2 tbsp of the butter in a wide frying pan and sauté the onion, green pepper, celery, garlic and bay leaf for 1–2 minutes, until hot and coated in butter.

COOK'S TIP: Be careful not to overcook the prawns as they will become tough.

3 Mix the cornflour and water to a smooth paste and stir it into the tomato sauce. Cook, stirring constantly, for about 2 minutes, then turn off the heat.

4 Melt the remaining butter in another frying pan and sauté the prawns, in batches, for 2–4 minutes, until pink and tender.

5 Reheat the tomato sauce, add the fried prawns and stir over the heat for 1 minute only. Check the seasoning and adjust if necessary. Serve immediately, accompanied by boiled rice garnished with parsley and shredded lemon peel, if liked.

Crab Bayou

This tasty supper dish can be made quickly and easily using fresh or frozen and thawed white crab meat.

Serves 6

INGREDIENTS

450 g/1 lb white crabmeat
3 hard-boiled egg yolks
5 ml/1 tsp Dijon mustard
75 g/3 oz/6 tbsp softened butter, plus
    extra for greasing
1.5 ml/¼ tsp cayenne pepper
45 ml/3 tbsp medium dry sherry
30 ml/2 tbsp finely chopped
    fresh parsley
120 ml/4 fl oz /½ cup whipping cream
40 g/1½ oz/½ cup thinly sliced
    spring onions (scallions), including
    some of the green stems
25 g/1 oz/½ cup dry breadcrumbs
salt and freshly ground
    black pepper
chives and parsley sprigs, to garnish

2 Put the egg yolks into a bowl and crumble with a fork. Add the mustard, 50 g/2 oz/¼ cup of the butter and the cayenne, and mash to a paste. Mash in the sherry and parsley.

3 Mix the cream and sliced spring onions into the bowl, then stir in the crab meat. Season to taste with salt and ground black pepper.

1 Preheat the oven to 180°C/350°F/ Gas 4. Pick over the crab meat and remove any shell or cartilage, keeping the pieces of crab as large as possible.

COOK'S TIP: For an attractive presentation, bake the Crab Bayou in scrubbed and greased scallop shells.

4 Divide the mixture among six greased ramekins or other small ovenproof dishes. Sprinkle the dry breadcrumbs on top of the mixture and dot with the remaining butter. Bake for about 20 minutes, until golden brown and bubbling. Serve immediately garnished with sprigs of fresh chives and parsley.

Blackened Chicken Breasts

Coated in a tantalizing array of aromatic spices, chicken fillets are fried at a very high heat in a modern Creole style.

Serves 6

INGREDIENTS
6 medium-size skinless chicken
  breast fillets
75 g/3 oz/6 tbsp butter
5 ml/1 tsp garlic powder
10 ml/2 tsp onion powder
5 ml/1 tsp cayenne pepper
10 ml/2 tsp mild paprika
7.5 ml/1½ tsp salt
2.5 ml/½ tsp freshly ground
  white pepper
5 ml/1 tsp freshly ground
  black pepper
1.5 ml/¼ tsp ground cumin
5 ml/1 teaspoon dried thyme
lettuce and salad vegetables, to serve
  (optional)

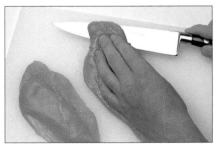

1 Slice each chicken breast fillet in half lengthways into two pieces of about the same thickness. Flatten the fillets slightly with the heel of your hand and place them in a large, shallow dish.

2 Melt the butter in a pan. Combine the garlic powder, onion powder, cayenne, paprika, salt, white pepper, black pepper, cumin and thyme in a small bowl.

3 Brush the chicken pieces on both sides with melted butter, then sprinkle them evenly with the spice mixture.

4 Heat a heavy-based frying pan over a high heat for 5–8 minutes, or until a drop of water sprinkled on the surface sizzles. Drizzle 5 ml/1 tsp of the melted butter over each chicken piece and place two or three of them in the frying pan.

VARIATION: Substitute six medium dog fish fillets for the chicken, but do not slice them in half. Cook for 2 minutes on one side and 1½–2 minutes on the other, or until the fish flakes easily.

5 Cook for 2-3 minutes, or until the undersides begin to blacken. Turn and cook the other side for 2–3 minutes more. Drain on kitchen paper and keep hot while you cook the remaining chicken pieces in the same way. Serve with lettuce and salad vegetables, if liked.

Chicken Sauce Piquante

This sauce goes with everything that runs, flies or swims in Louisiana — you will even find alligator sauce piquante on menus.

Serves 4

INGREDIENTS

4 chicken legs or 2 legs and 2 breasts
75 ml/5 tbsp vegetable oil
50 g/2 oz/½ cup plain (all-purpose) flour
1 medium onion, chopped
2 celery sticks, sliced
1 green (bell) pepper, seeded and diced
2 garlic cloves, crushed
1 bay leaf
2.5 ml/½ tsp dried thyme
2.5 ml/½ tsp dried oregano
1–2 fresh red chillies, seeded and
    finely chopped
400 g/14 oz can tomatoes, chopped,
    with their juice
300 ml/½ pint/1¼ cups chicken stock
salt and freshly ground
    black pepper
watercress or rocket (arugula), to garnish
boiled potatoes tossed in butter
    and chopped fresh parsley,
    to serve

1 Halve the chicken legs through the joint, or the breasts across the middle, to give eight pieces.

2 Heat the oil in a heavy-based frying pan and fry the chicken pieces until browned on all sides. Remove from the pan with a slotted spoon and set aside while you prepare the sauce.

3 Strain the oil into a heavy-based, flameproof casserole. Set over a low heat and stir in the flour. Cook, stirring constantly with a spoon or whisk until the roux is a golden brown colour.

4 Immediately, add the prepared onion, celery and green pepper to the roux, and continue to stir over a low heat for 2–3 minutes.

5 Add the garlic, bay leaf, thyme, oregano and chillies. Stir for 1 minute over a medium heat, then lower the heat and stir in the tomatoes with their juice.

5 Increase the heat slightly and gradually stir in the stock. Add the chicken, cover and simmer for 5 minutes, or until the chicken is tender. If there is too much sauce or it is too runny, remove the lid for the last 10–15 minutes of cooking time and increase the heat slightly.

7 Check the seasoning and serve hot, garnished with watercress or rocket and accompanied by boiled potatoes.

VARIATION: For a milder sauce, use one chilli and add a dash of Tabasco, or to taste, at the end.

37

Chicken Jambalaya

The name comes from the French for 'jumble', and jambalayas are a colourful mixture of highly flavoured ingredients. They are always made in large quantities for big family or celebration meals.

Serves 10

INGREDIENTS
2 x 1.3 kg/3 lb chickens
450 g/1 lb piece raw smoked gammon
50 g/2 oz/¼ cup lard or bacon fat
50 g/2 oz/½ cup plain (all-purpose) flour
3 medium onions, thinly sliced
2 green (bell) peppers, seeded and sliced
675 g/1½ lb tomatoes, peeled and chopped
2–3 garlic cloves, crushed
10 ml/2 tsp chopped fresh thyme or
    5 ml/1 tsp dried thyme
24 peeled, raw prawns (jumbo shrimp)
500 g/1¼ lb/3 cups long grain rice
1 litre/1¾ pints/4 cups water
2–3 dashes of Tabasco sauce
1 bunch spring onions (scallions), chopped
45 ml/3 tbsp chopped fresh parsley
salt and freshly ground black pepper

2 Melt the lard or bacon fat in a large, heavy-based pan or flameproof casserole. Fry the chicken pieces until browned all over. Remove with a slotted spoon and set aside.

3 Lower the heat, sprinkle in the flour and stir constantly until the roux turns a light golden brown.

4 Return the chicken pieces to the pan, add the diced gammon, onions, green peppers, tomatoes, garlic and thyme and cook, stirring frequently, for 10 minutes.

1 Cut each chicken into 10 pieces and season with salt and pepper. Dice the gammon, discarding the rind and fat.

5 Stir in the prawns, then stir in the rice and add the water. Season to taste with salt, pepper and Tabasco. Bring to the boil and cook over a low heat until the rice is tender and the liquid has been absorbed. Add a little boiling water if the rice looks like drying out before it is cooked.

6 Reserve a little of the chopped spring onions and parsley for the garnish and stir the remainder into the jambalaya. Serve piping hot with the reserved spring onions and parsley scattered over the top of each portion.

Poussins with Dirty Rice

The rice is not, of course, dirty. It is so called because it is jazzed up with a variety of ingredients – and jazz was called 'dirty music'.

Serves 4

INGREDIENTS
4 poussins (spring chickens)
2 bay leaves, halved
25 g/1 oz/2 tbsp butter
juice of 1 lemon
salt and freshly ground black pepper

FOR THE RICE
60 ml/4 tbsp vegetable oil
25 g/1 oz/¼ cup plain (all-purpose) flour
50 g/2 oz/¼ cup butter
1 large onion, chopped
2 celery sticks, chopped
1 green (bell) pepper, seeded and diced
2 garlic cloves, crushed
200 g/7 oz minced (ground) pork
225 g/8 oz chicken livers, trimmed
    and sliced
dash of Tabasco sauce
300 ml/½ pint/1¼ cups chicken stock
4 spring onions (scallions), shredded
45 ml/3 tbsp chopped fresh parsley
225 g/8 oz/generous 1 cup long grain
    rice, cooked

1 First, prepare the roux. Heat 30 ml/ 2 tbsp of the oil in a small, heavy-based pan. Add the flour and cook over a low heat, stirring constantly with a wooden spoon or whisk until the roux is a golden brown colour. Remove the pan from the heat and place immediately on a cold surface.

2 Heat the remaining oil with the butter in a frying pan and stir-fry the onion, celery and green pepper for about 5 minutes, or until softened. Add the garlic and pork and stir-fry, breaking up the pork, for 5 minutes, or until browned.

3 Add the sliced chicken livers and fry for 2–3 minutes, or until they have changed colour all over. Add a dash of Tabasco and season with salt and black pepper to taste.

4 Stir the roux into the mixture, then gradually stir in the stock. Bring to simmering point, cover and simmer, stirring occasionally, for 30 minutes. Uncover the pan and cook, stirring frequently, for a further 15 minutes.

5 Preheat the oven to 200°C/400°F/ Gas 6. Mix the spring onions and parsley into the meat mixture. Put the cooked rice into a large bowl and stir in the meat mixture.

6 Put ½ bay leaf and 15 ml/1 tbsp of the rice mixture into the cavity of each poussin. Rub the outside with the butter and season with salt and freshly ground black pepper.

7 Put the birds on a rack in a roasting pan and sprinkle them with the lemon juice. Roast for 35–40 minutes, basting twice with the pan juices.

8 Put the remaining rice into a shallow, ovenproof dish, cover and place on a low shelf in the oven for the last 15–20 minutes of the poussins' cooking time.

9 Divide the rice among four plates and place a poussin on each. Skim the fat from the roasting juices and pour them over the birds. Serve immediately.

Roast Pork with Cajun Stuffing

The familiar trinity of onion, celery and green pepper gives Cajun flavour to a handsome roast complete with crackling.

Serves 6

INGREDIENTS
1.5 kg/3½ lb boned loin of pork
15 ml/1 tbsp salt
5 ml/1 tsp each freshly ground black
    pepper, cayenne pepper, paprika and
    dried oregano
30 ml/2 tbsp vegetable oil or
    25 g/1 oz/2 tbsp lard
1 small onion, finely chopped
1 celery stick, finely chopped
½ green (bell) pepper, finely chopped
1 garlic clove, crushed

2 Preheat the oven to 220°C/425°F/ Gas 7. In a bowl, combine the ground black pepper, cayenne, paprika and oregano with the remaining salt and rub this mixture over the fleshy side of the meat.

1 If the pork is tied up, untie it. Score the skin closely, Rub 10 ml/2 tsp of the salt into the skin, preferably the night before, or, if not, as far in advance of cooking as possible on the day. Bring the pork to room temperature.

3 Heat the oil or lard and gently fry the chopped onion, celery and green pepper for 4 minutes, then add the crushed garlic and fry for 1 minute more. Spread the vegetables over the flesh side of the meat and roll up the pork, skin-side out. Tie securely with string in several places.

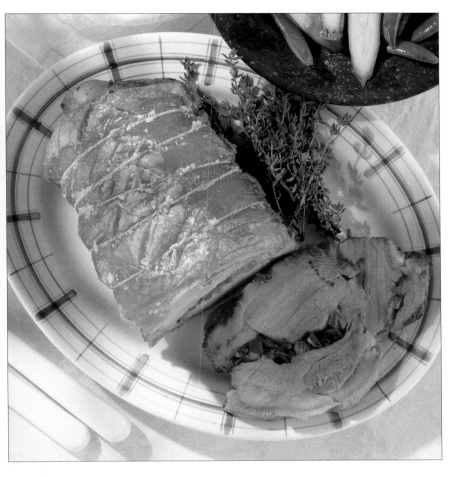

4 Place the meat on a rack in a roasting pan and roast for 30 minutes. Reduce the oven temperature to 180°C/350°F/Gas 4 and roast for a further 1½ hours, basting with the pan juices every 15–20 minutes. If the crackling is not becoming crisp and bubbly towards the end of cooking, increase the oven temperature for the last 20–30 minutes.

5 Allow the meat to rest for about 10 minutes before carving. Serve hot.

COOK'S TIP: You can roast potatoes or sweet potatoes in the tin with the meat or bake them in their skins in the oven. Use the pan juices with some red wine and a bay leaf to make a gravy.

Pork Chops with Lemon & Garlic Grilling Sauce

This spicy sauce is absolutely delicious whether the chops are grilled conventionally or cooked on a barbecue.

Serves 4

INGREDIENTS
4 pork chops
115 g/4 oz/½ cup butter
½ lemon
15 ml/1 tbsp Worcestershire sauce
7.5 ml/1½ tsp Tabasco sauce
1 garlic clove, finely chopped
salt and freshly ground black pepper
chargrilled vegetables, to serve

1 Preheat the grill (broiler). Put the chops in the grill pan and set aside.

2 Melt the butter in a small, non-aluminium frying pan, add the lemon juice and bring to simmering point.

COOK'S TIP: This flavoured butter is equally good with chicken pieces, duck breasts or lamb steaks and also works well with vegetables.

3 Add the Worcestershire and Tabasco sauces and the garlic and cook over a low heat, without browning the garlic, for about 5 minutes. Season to taste.

4 Brush the chops with the flavoured butter and cook under the grill for 5 minutes. Turn and brush with more butter, then grill (broil) for a further 5 minutes, or until cooked through and tender.

5 Serve with a little of the flavoured butter trickled over and accompanied by chargrilled vegetables.

Green Herb Gumbo

Traditionally served at the end of Lent, this is a joyful, sweetly spiced and revitalizing dish, even if you haven't been fasting.

Serves 6–8

INGREDIENTS
350 g/12 oz piece raw smoked gammon
25 g/1 oz/2 tbsp lard or 30 ml/2 tbsp
  vegetable oil
1 large Spanish onion,
  roughly chopped
2–3 garlic cloves, crushed
5 ml/1 tsp dried oregano
5 ml/1 tsp dried thyme
2 bay leaves
2 cloves
2 celery sticks, sliced
1 green (bell) pepper, seeded
  and chopped
½ medium green cabbage,
  finely shredded
2 litres/3½ pints/9 cups chicken or
  vegetable stock or water
200 g/7 oz kale, or spring greens
  (collards) finely shredded
200 g/7 oz Chinese leaves (Chinese
  cabbage), finely shredded
200 g/7 oz spinach, shredded
6 spring onions (scallions), finely
  shredded
25 g/1 oz/½ cup chopped
  fresh parsley
2.5 ml/½ tsp ground allspice
¼ nutmeg, grated
salt, freshly ground black pepper and
  cayenne pepper
warm French bread or garlic
  bread, to serve

1 Dice the gammon finely, reserving any fat and the rind in one piece. Put the fat piece with the lard or oil into a deep pan and heat until it sizzles. Add the gammon, onion, garlic, oregano and thyme and stir over a medium heat for 5 minutes.

2 Add the bay leaves, cloves, celery and green pepper and cook, stirring, for 3 minutes. Add the cabbage and stock or water. Bring to the boil, lower the heat and simmer for 5 minutes.

3 Add the spring greens or kale and Chinese leaves, bring to the boil and cook for 2 minutes.

4 Add the spinach and spring onions, lower the heat and simmer for 1 minute. Add the parsley, allspice and nutmeg, and season with salt, pepper and cayenne to taste.

5 Remove and discard the gammon fat and cloves. Serve the gumbo immediately with warm bread.

COOK'S TIP: Chinese mustard cabbage is widely available in supermarkets and Chinese food stores. If you can't find it, you can substitute turnip tops or kohlrabi leaves.

Corn Maque Choux

An ideal medley for grills.

Serves 4

INGREDIENTS
30 ml/2 tbsp groundnut or olive oil
1 onion, very finely chopped
1 celery stick, very finely chopped
½ small green (bell) pepper, seeded and
    finely chopped
450 g/1 lb/2⅔ cups corn kernels
    (fresh, frozen or canned)
2.5 ml/½ tsp cayenne pepper
120 ml/4 fl oz/½ cup white wine
    or water
1 medium tomato, diced
5 ml/1 tsp salt
45 ml/3 tbsp whipping cream
30 ml/2 tbsp shredded fresh basil
freshly ground black pepper

1 Heat the oil in a heavy-based pan
and fry the onion over a low heat,
stirring occasionally, for 8–10 minutes.
Increase the heat and add the celery
and green pepper. Cook, stirring
constantly, for 5 minutes.

2 Stir in the sweetcorn and cayenne
and cook for 10 minutes.

3 Stir in the wine or water. Add the
tomato, salt and pepper. Stir, cover and
cook over a low heat for 8–10 minutes.
Off the heat, stir in the cream and
basil. Serve immediately.

Spring Greens & Rice

Delicious with hearty stews.

Serves 4

INGREDIENTS
475 ml/16 fl oz/2 cups chicken stock
200 g/7 oz/1 cup long grain rice
15 g/½ oz/1 tbsp butter
2.5 ml/½ tsp salt
350 g/12 oz spring greens (collards)
freshly ground black pepper

1 Bring the stock to the boil in a
medium pan. Add the rice, butter and
salt and stir.

2 Shred the spring greens, and add to
the pan.

3 Bring the rice mixture back to the
boil, lower the heat, cover and cook for
15-20 minutes, or until the rice is
tender. Season with freshly ground black
pepper to taste and serve immediately.

Right: Corn Maque Choux (top);
Spring Greens & Rice

Spiced Fried Aubergine

Serve these crisp, cornmeal-coated aubergine slices with grilled fish or poultry or with a salad as a vegetarian dish.

Serves 3–4

INGREDIENTS
1 large aubergine (eggplant)
1 egg
120 ml/4 fl oz/½ cup whole milk
2.5 ml/½ tsp paprika
2.5 ml/½ tsp cayenne pepper
2.5 ml/½ tsp freshly ground black pepper
2.5 ml/½ tsp garlic salt
115 g/4 oz/1 cup fine cornmeal
oil, for deep-frying
salt

1 Cut the aubergine into 1 cm/½ in thick slices. Sprinkle with salt and stack them in a colander. Set aside to drain for 30 minutes, then rinse and pat dry with kitchen paper.

2 Beat together the egg, milk, paprika, cayenne, black pepper and garlic salt in a shallow dish. Spread out the cornmeal on a plate. Heat the oil in a large frying pan.

3 Coat each aubergine slice in the egg mixture, shaking off the excess, and then dip in the cornmeal to coat evenly. As soon as a slice is coated, drop it into the hot oil.

4 Fry three or four slices at a time, turning once, until golden brown and crispy on both sides. Drain well on kitchen paper and keep warm until all the slices are fried. Serve hot.

Baked Sweet Potatoes

Sweet potatoes go well with the favourite Cajun seasonings – salt, black and white pepper, and cayenne.

Serves 3–6

INGREDIENTS

3 orange-fleshed sweet potatoes, about 450 g/1 lb each
75 g/3 oz/6 tbsp butter, sliced
cayenne pepper
salt and freshly ground black and freshly ground white pepper

1 Wash the potatoes, leaving the skins wet. Rub salt into the skins, prick with a fork all over and place in the oven. Set the oven to 200°C/400°F/Gas 6. (Sweet potatoes cook quickly; there is no need to preheat the oven.)

2 Bake for 1 hour, until the flesh yields and feels soft when pressed.

3 To serve in halves as an accompaniment, cut each in half lengthways and make close diagonal cuts in the flesh of each half. Spread with slices of butter, working the butter and seasonings into the cuts with a knife point.

4 To serve whole, make an incision along the length of each potato. Open slightly and put in slices of butter along the length. Season with salt and the peppers.

Vinegared Chilli Cabbage

A tasty boost for cabbage.

Serves 4–6

INGREDIENTS
1 fresh red chilli, halved, seeded
  and shredded
25 g/1 oz/2 tbsp lard or butter
2 garlic cloves, crushed
1 medium white cabbage, shredded
75 ml/5 tbsp water
10 ml/2 tsp cider vinegar
5 ml/1 tsp cayenne pepper
salt

1 Put the chilli and lard or butter
in a large pan and cook over a
medium heat until the chilli sizzles
and curls at the edges.

2 Add the garlic and cabbage and stir
until the cabbage is coated. Add salt
and the water. Bring to the boil,
cover and lower the heat.

3 Cook, shaking the pan frequently,
for 3–4 minutes, or until the cabbage
has wilted. Remove the lid, increase
the heat and cook until all the liquid
has evaporated. Check the seasoning,
adding more salt if necessary. Sprinkle
the cider vinegar and cayenne over the
cabbage and serve.

*Right: Vinegared Chilli Cabbage (top);
Coleslaw in Hot Dressing*

Coleslaw in Hot Dressing

An unusual buffet salad.

Serves 6

INGREDIENTS
½ white cabbage, cored and shredded
2 celery sticks, thinly sliced
1 green (bell) pepper, thinly sliced
4 spring onions (scallions), shredded
pinch of cayenne pepper

FOR THE DRESSING
15 ml/1 tbsp Dijon mustard
10 ml/2 tsp creamed horseradish
5 ml/1 tsp Tabasco sauce
30 ml/2 tbsp red wine vinegar
75 ml/5 tbsp olive oil
salt and freshly ground black pepper

1 Mix together the cabbage, celery,
green pepper and spring onions in a
large salad bowl.

2 Make the dressing. Mix together
the mustard, horseradish and Tabasco
in a small bowl. Gradually stir in the
vinegar with a fork, then beat in the
oil and season to taste with salt and
pepper. Pour the dressing on the salad
and toss well. Leave to stand for at
least 1 hour, turning the salad once or
twice during this time.

3 Immediately before serving, season
the salad if necessary, toss again and
sprinkle with cayenne.

Creamy Potato Salad

Great with a bowl of gumbo or with grills and cold meats.

Serves 6–8

INGREDIENTS
8 medium-sized waxy potatoes
1 green (bell) pepper, seeded and diced
1 large pickled gherkin, chopped
4 spring onions (scallions), sliced
3 hard-boiled eggs, chopped
250 ml/8 fl oz/1 cup mayonnaise
15 ml/1 tbsp Dijon mustard
Tabasco sauce
cayenne pepper (optional)
salt and freshly ground black pepper

1 Cook the potatoes in their skins in lightly salted boiling water until tender. Drain, and when cool enough to handle, peel and coarsely dice.

2 Put the potatoes in a salad bowl and mix with the green pepper, gherkin, spring onions and hard-boiled eggs.

3 Mix the mayonnaise with the mustard in a separate bowl and season to taste with Tabasco, salt and pepper.

4 Add the dressing to the salad and toss gently. Sprinkle a pinch of cayenne on top, if you like, and serve.

Right: Creamy Potato Salad (top); Smothered Okra

Smothered Okra

Choose small, firm okra for this scrumptious dish.

Serves 4–6

INGREDIENTS
500 g/1¼ lb okra
25 g/1 oz/2 tbsp butter
1 red onion, thinly sliced
1 garlic clove, crushed
4 large tomatoes, peeled, seeded
   and chopped
5 ml/1 tsp red wine vinegar
120 ml/4 fl oz/½ cup water
cayenne pepper
salt and freshly ground black pepper

1 Wash and dry the okra and then trim, cutting the stem end of each one just level with the pod.

2 Melt the butter in a medium pan and fry the onion over a low heat, stirring frequently, for 5–10 minutes. Add the garlic and cook, stirring, for 1 minute, then add the tomatoes, vinegar and water. Add salt and cook, uncovered until the mixture thickens.

3 Stir in the okra, cover and cook over a very low heat for about 25 minutes, checking halfway through and adding a little water if the sauce is drying out. When the okra are quite soft, season to taste with cayenne and black pepper. Serve hot.

Bread Pudding with Cranberry Sauce

The sharpness of cranberries contrasts beautifully with the sweetness of this substantial Louisiana pudding.

Serves 6–8

INGREDIENTS
50 g/2 oz/¼ cup butter, melted
750 ml/1¼ pints/3 cups milk
3 eggs
90 g/3½ oz/½ cup caster (superfine)
  sugar
5 ml/1 tsp vanilla extract
10 ml/2 tsp ground cinnamon
½ nutmeg
400 g/14 oz/9 cups cubed bread
  cut from a day-old French loaf
  (including crusts)
50 g/2 oz/⅓ cup chopped walnuts
75 g/3 oz/½ cup sultanas
  (golden raisins)

FOR THE CRANBERRY SAUCE
350 g/12 oz/3 cups cranberries,
  fresh or frozen
finely grated rind and juice of 1
  large orange
25 g/1 oz/ 2 tbsp caster (superfine)
  sugar

1 Swirl the butter around a deep, ovenproof pie dish to coat it generously. Tip any excess into the milk. Beat the eggs until light and frothy, then beat in the sugar, vanilla extract and cinnamon. Grate in the nutmeg, then mix in the milk.

2 Pack the cubed French bread into the pie dish. Then scatter the chopped walnuts and the sultanas between the layers.

3 Pour the spiced egg mixture evenly over the bread, nuts and fruit, and set aside for 45 minutes.

4 Preheat the oven to 180°C/350°F/ Gas 4 and bake the pudding for 45 minutes, until risen and puffy. Increase the temperature to 200°C/ 400°F/Gas 6 for the last 10–15 minutes if the top is not turning golden.

5 To make the cranberry sauce, put the cranberries, grated orange rind and juice and sugar into a medium pan. Cook, stirring constantly, over a low heat until the sugar has dissolved. Cook until the berries pop but retain their shape and the mixture thickens to the consistency of jam. Serve with the pudding, either hot or cold.

French Quarter Beignets

Flavoured with cinnamon, these elegant, little deep-fried pastries are a tempting treat at any time of day.

Makes about 20

INGREDIENTS
225 g/8 oz/2 cups plain (all-purpose)
   flour, plus extra for dusting
5 ml/1 tsp salt
15 ml/1 tbsp baking powder
5 ml/1 tsp ground cinnamon
2 eggs
50 g/2 oz/¼ cup caster (superfine) sugar
175 ml/6 fl oz/¾ cup whole milk
2.5 ml/½ tsp vanilla extract
vegetable oil, for deep-frying
icing (confectioners') sugar, to dust

2 Beat together the eggs, sugar, milk and vanilla extract in another bowl. Pour the egg mixture into the dry ingredients and mix quickly to form a dough. Turn the dough on to a lightly floured surface and knead until smooth and elastic.

1 Sift the flour, salt, baking powder and ground cinnamon together in a medium bowl.

COOK'S TIP: Try serving these pastries with a fruit or nut ice cream or Bananas Foster, or simply enjoy with a cup of coffee.

3 Heat the oil for deep-frying to 190°C/375°F or until a cube of day-old bread browns in 30 seconds. Meanwhile, roll out the dough to a 5 mm/¼ in thick round. Slice it diagonally into diamonds about 7.5 cm/3 in long.

4 Fry the beignets in the oil, in batches, until golden brown all over. Remove with tongs or a slotted spoon and drain on kitchen paper. Sprinkle with icing sugar before serving warm or cold.

Bananas Foster

Dick Foster was on the Vice Committee in charge of cleaning up the French Quarter of New Orleans in the 1950s.

Serves 4

INGREDIENTS
75 g/3 oz/⅓ cup soft light brown sugar
2.5 ml/½ tsp ground cinnamon
2.5 ml/½ tsp freshly grated nutmeg
50 g/2 oz/¼ cup butter
60 ml/4 tbsp banana liqueur
75 ml/5 tbsp dark rum
4 firm bananas
4 scoops vanilla ice cream

1 Combine the sugar, cinnamon and nutmeg. Melt the butter in a heavy frying pan and add the sugar mixture. Add the liqueur and rum and stir over the heat until the sauce is syrupy.

2 Peel the bananas, slice in half lenthways and add to the pan, turning to coat with the sauce. Set the sauce alight with a long taper.

3 When the flames have died down, divide the banana slices among four serving plates and add a scoop of ice cream. Pour the sauce over them and serve immediately.

VARIATION: Try serving the bananas with praline or walnut ice cream instead. You can also serve with crème fraîche or cream.

Creole Ambrosia

This refreshing, cold, fruity dessert is easy to make – and even easier to eat – at any time of year.

Serves 6

INGREDIENTS
6 oranges
1 fresh whole coconut
25 g/1 oz/2 tbsp caster (superfine) sugar

1 Peel the oranges, removing all the white pith, then slice thinly, picking out the pips with the point of the knife. Do this on a plate to catch the juice.

2 Pierce the 'eyes' of the coconut and pour away the milk. Crack open the coconut with a hammer. (Put it inside a plastic bag to avoid flying chips of shell. It is also best done outside on a stone surface.)

3 Peel the coconut with a sharp knife, then coarsely grate half the flesh with a hand grater or in a food processor. (Use the remaining half for another dish.)

4 Layer the grated coconut and orange slices in a glass bowl, sprinkling a little sugar and reserved orange juice over each layer of oranges.

5 Set aside for 2 hours before serving either at room temperature or chilled.

VARIATION: Substituting mangoes for the oranges makes the dessert more exotic, but less authentic.

Pecan Nut Divinity Cake

This, nutty-flavoured rich layer cake is so divine that it is almost sinful.
When the icing is ready to use, you need to work quickly before it sets.

Serves 6–8

INGREDIENTS
275 g/10 oz/1⅔ cups pecan nuts
350 g/12 oz/3 cups plain (all-purpose)
    flour
7.5 ml/1½ tsp baking powder
2.5 ml/½ tsp salt
225 g/8 oz/1 cup unsalted (sweet) butter,
    at room temperature
400 g/14 oz/2 cups caster (superfine)
    sugar
5 eggs
250 ml/8 fl oz/1 cup whole milk
5 ml/1 tsp vanilla extract

FOR THE DIVINITY ICING
350 g/12 oz/3 cups
    icing (confectioners') sugar
3 egg whites, at room temperature
2 drops of vanilla extract

1 Toast the pecans, in batches, in a
heavy-based pan over a high heat,
tossing them frequently, until they
darken. Cool then chop coarsely.

2 Preheat the oven to 180°C/350°F/
Gas 4. Oil and lightly flour three
23 cm/9 in diameter cake tins. Sift the
flour, baking powder and salt together.
Toss half the toasted pecans in 30 ml/
2 tbsp of the flour mixture, reserving
the remainder.

3 Cream the butter and sugar
together until pale and fluffy. Add the
eggs, one at a time, beating well after
each addition. Mix together the milk
and vanilla extract. Stir the flour into
the creamed mixture in three batches,
alternating with the milk. Finally, fold
in the floured nuts.

4 Pour the cake mixture into the
prepared tins and bake for 30 minutes,
or until the tops are golden and the
sides have come away slightly from
the tins. Remove from the oven and
leave to cool in the tins for 5 minutes
before turning out on to wire racks to
cool completely.

5 To make the icing, sift the icing
sugar into a heatproof bowl, add the
eggs whites and set the bowl over a
pan of simmering water. Whisk for
5–10 minutes, or until stiff peaks form.
Add the vanilla extract. Remove the
bowl from the heat and continue
whisking for a further 2–3 minutes.

6 Working quickly, spread the cake layers with some of the divinity icing, and sprinkle each layer with some of the reserved toasted pecans. Carefully sandwich the cake layers together, then ice the sides of the assembled cake with the remaining icing.

Index

This edition is published by Lorenz Books,
an imprint of Anness Publishing Ltd,
108 Great Russell Street, London WC1B 3NA info@anness.com
www.annesspublishing.com; twitter: @Anness_Books

© Anness Publishing Limited 2015

If you like the images in this book and would like to investigate using them for publishing, promotions or advertising, please visit our website www.practicalpictures.com for more information.

Publisher: Joanna Lorenz
Editor: Valerie Ferguson & Helen Sudell
Production Controller: Rosanna Anness

Recipes contributed by: Carla Capalbo, Ruby Le Bois, and Laura Washburn.

Photography: James Duncan and Amanda Heywood.

A CIP catalogue record for this book is available from the British Library

Cook's Notes

Bracketed terms are intended for American readers.

For all recipes, quantities are given in both metric and imperial measures and, where appropriate, in standard cups and spoons. Follow one set of measures, but not a mixture.

Standard spoon and cup measures are level. 1 tsp = 5ml, 1 tbsp = 15ml, 1 cup = 250ml/ 8fl oz. Australian standard tablespoons are 20ml. Australian readers should use 3 tsp in place of 1 tbsp for measuring small quantities.

American pints are 16fl oz/2 cups. American readers should use 20fl oz/2.5 cups in place of 1 pint when measuring liquids.

Electric oven temperatures in this book are for conventional ovens. When using a fan oven, the temperature will probably need to be reduced by about 10–20°C/20–40°F. Check with your manufacturer's instruction book for guidance.

Medium (US large) eggs are used unless otherwise stated.